Antarctic Circle

King Haakon VII Sea

SOUTHERN
OCEAN

THE
SOUTH POLE

East Antarctic
Ice Sheet

Ronne Ice
Shelf

Bellinghausen
Sea

West Antarctic
Ice Sheet

+ South Pole

Ross Ice
Shelf

Ross
Sea

By Todd Bluthenthal

Gareth Stevens
PUBLISHING

Please visit our website, www.garethstevens.com. For a free color catalog of all our high-quality books, call toll free 1-800-542-2595 or fax 1-877-542-2596.

Cataloging-in-Publication Data
Names: Bluthenthal, Todd.
Title: The South Pole / Todd Bluthenthal.
Description: New York : Gareth Stevens Publishing, 2018. | Series: Where on Earth? mapping parts of the world | Includes index.
Identifiers: ISBN 9781482464337 (pbk.) | ISBN 9781482464351 (library bound) | ISBN 9781482464344 (6 pack)
Subjects: LCSH: Antarctica–Juvenile literature. | South Pole–Juvenile literature.
Classification: LCC G863.B58 2018 | DDC 919.89–dc23

Published in 2018 by
Gareth Stevens Publishing
111 East 14th Street, Suite 349
New York, NY 10003

Designer: Samantha DeMartin
Editor: Joan Stoltman

Photo credits: Series art CHAPLIA YAROSLAV/Shutterstock.com; cover, p. 1 (photo) Volodymyr/Shutterstock.com; cover, p. 1 (map) Rainer Lesniewski/Shutterstock.com; p. 5 vinz89/Shutterstock.com; p. 7 Anton_Ivanov/Shutterstock.com; p. 9 Wojciech Dziadosz/Shutterstock.com; p. 11 Designua/Shutterstock.com; p. 13 Istimages/ Shutterstock.com; p. 15 Peter Hermes Furian/Shutterstock.com; p. 17 Historical/Corbis Historical/Getty Images; p. 19 George Burba/Shutterstock.com; p. 21 bikeriderlondon/Shutterstock.com.

Printed in the United States of America

CPSIA compliance information: Batch #CS17GS: For further information contact Gareth Stevens, New York, New York at 1-800-542-2595.

CONTENTS

Boldface words appear in the glossary.

What Is the South Pole?

The South Pole is the southernmost point on Earth. When you are standing at the South Pole, any other place on Earth is north of you! The South Pole is found on the **continent** of Antarctica.

South Pole

Antarctica

5

All About Antarctica

Antarctica is surrounded by the Southern Ocean. It's the coldest, windiest place on Earth. Huge ice sheets cover almost all Antarctica. The ice can be anywhere from 1 to 3 miles (1.6 to 4.8 km) thick!

7

The South Pole Climate

The South Pole's **climate** is cold and dry. The coldest **temperature** ever recorded on Earth happened near there. It was –135.8°F (–94.7°C) in August 2010! There's so little rain in Antarctica that it's called a cold desert. In fact, it's the driest desert on Earth!

9

The South Pole has two seasons. Earth's **axis** is **tilted** as it moves around the sun throughout the year. In summer, the tilt brings a little sun to Antarctica. It warms to a temperature of –18°F (–28°C). In winter, no sun reaches the South Pole!

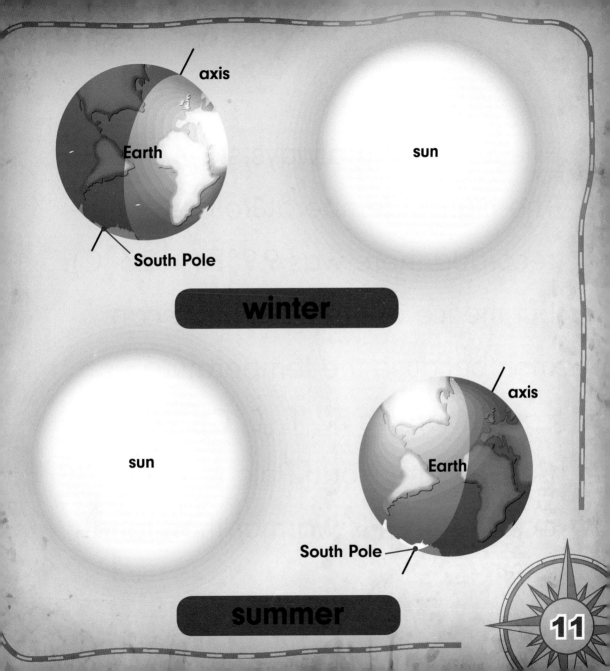

axis

Earth

South Pole

sun

winter

sun

axis

Earth

South Pole

summer

The South Pole always stays frozen. The highest temperature ever recorded there was 9.9°F (-12.3°C). But the ice at the North Pole can melt because the temperature can get above 32°F (0°C)! Why? Because the North Pole is in the ocean, which is warmer than land!

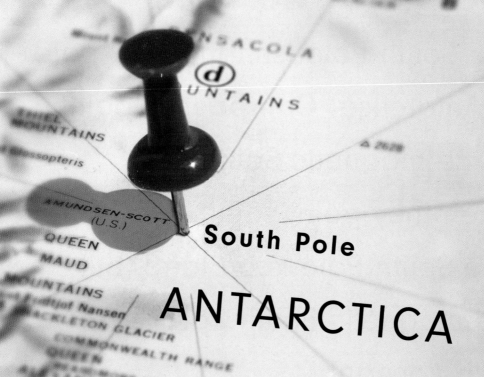

There Are Two South Poles?

The South Pole isn't the only pole in Antarctica! **Compasses** point to the magnetic South Pole when they point south. The true South Pole is on land, but the magnetic South Pole is in the ocean!

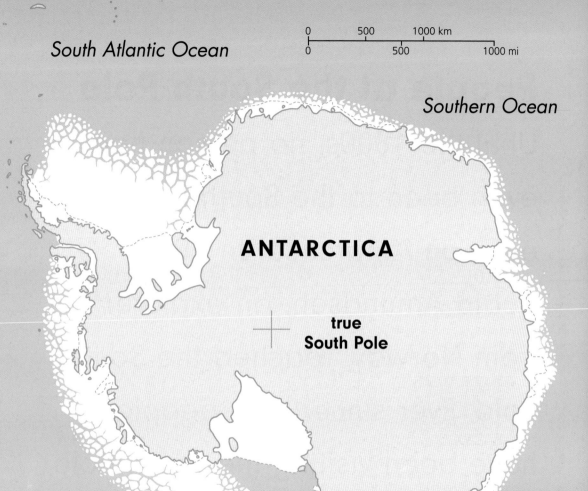

South Atlantic Ocean

Southern Ocean

ANTARCTICA

true
South Pole

magnetic
South Pole

Southern Ocean

0   500   1000 km
0   500   1000 mi

15

People at the South Pole

Until the 1800s, no person had even been to the South Pole or even on Antarctica! In 1911, Roald Amundsen, an explorer from Norway, reached the South Pole. Ever since then, people have been visiting the South Pole and Antarctica!

Roald Amundsen

17

Scientists visit the area around the South Pole to study everything from the ocean to the stars. It's not easy to visit, though! Everything, including food and clothing, is brought on planes, trucks, helicopters, and snow tractors during summer.

19

Animals at the South Pole

The South Pole is home to many land and sea animals, such as penguins, seals, **squids**, and whales. These animals have special fur, feathers, skin, and fat that help them stay warm in this cold climate!

GLOSSARY

axis: an imaginary straight line around which a planet turns

climate: the average weather conditions of a place over time

compass: a tool for finding directions

continent: one of Earth's seven great landmasses

squid: an underwater animal that is somewhat like an octopus

temperature: how hot or cold something is

tilted: slanted, not straight up and down

FOR MORE INFORMATION

BOOKS

Besel, Jennifer M. *The Coldest Places on Earth*. Mankato, MN: Capstone Press, 2010.

Parker, Victoria. *How Far Is Far? Comparing Geographical Distances*. Chicago, IL: Heinemann Library, 2011.

Waldron, Melanie. *Polar Regions*. Chicago, IL: Capstone Raintree, 2013.

WEBSITES

Antarctica
timeforkids.com/minisite/antarctica
Read all sorts of articles about Antarctica.

Become an Antarctic Explorer with Panoramic Imagery
googleblog.blogspot.com/2012/07/become-antarctic-explorer-with.html
Check out this photograph at the South Pole, which shows what it looks like in every direction!

INDEX